# Practice Paper 1

# Non-Verbal Reasoning

## Read the following carefully:

1. **Do not open or turn over the page in this booklet until you are told to do so.**

2. This is a multiple-choice test in which you have to mark your answer to each question on the answer sheet. You should mark only one answer for each question.

3. Draw a firm line clearly through the rectangle next to your answer like this ▭. If you make a mistake, rub it out as completely as you can and put in your new answer.

4. There are two sections in this test. Each section starts with an explanation of what to do, followed by a worked example with the answer marked on the answer sheet. Each section also contains some practice questions.

5. Be sure to keep your place in the correct section on the answer sheet. Mark your answer in the box that has the same number as the test question.

6. You may not be able to finish all the questions, but try to do as many as you can. If you cannot do a question, do not waste time on it but go on to the next. If you are not sure of an answer, choose the one you think is best.

7. You may do any rough working on a separate sheet of paper.

8. **Work as quickly and as carefully as you can.**

On the left in the example below, there are two figures that are alike. On the right, there are five more figures: one of these is **most like** the two figures on the left and its letter has been marked on your answer sheet.

**Example**

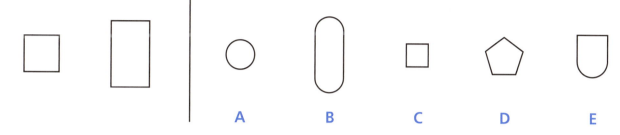

**Answer: C**

Now do the two practice questions below.
**Mark the correct answers on your answer sheet.**

## P1

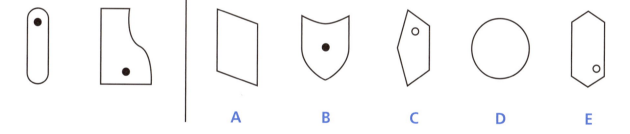

## P2

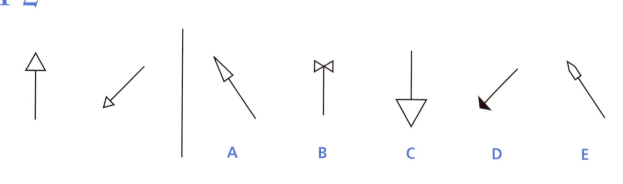

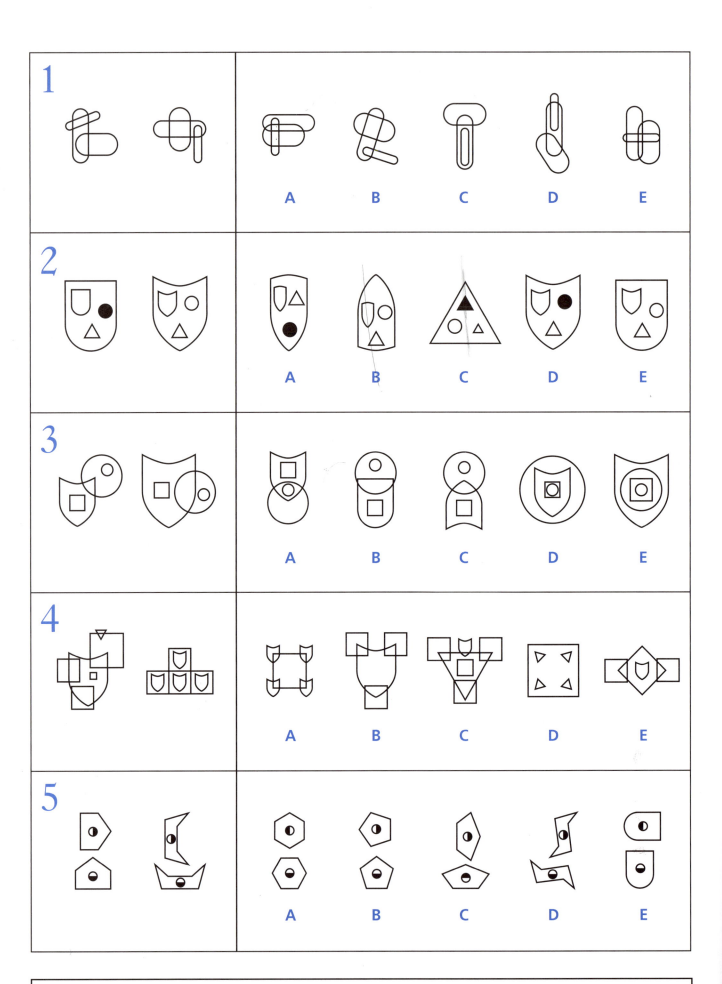

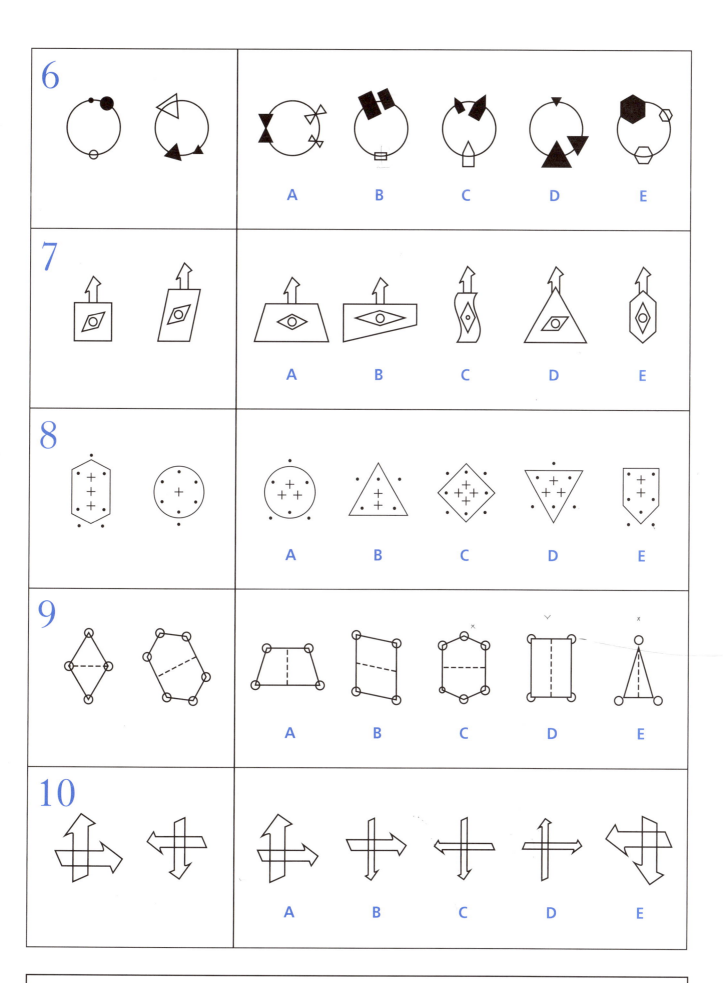

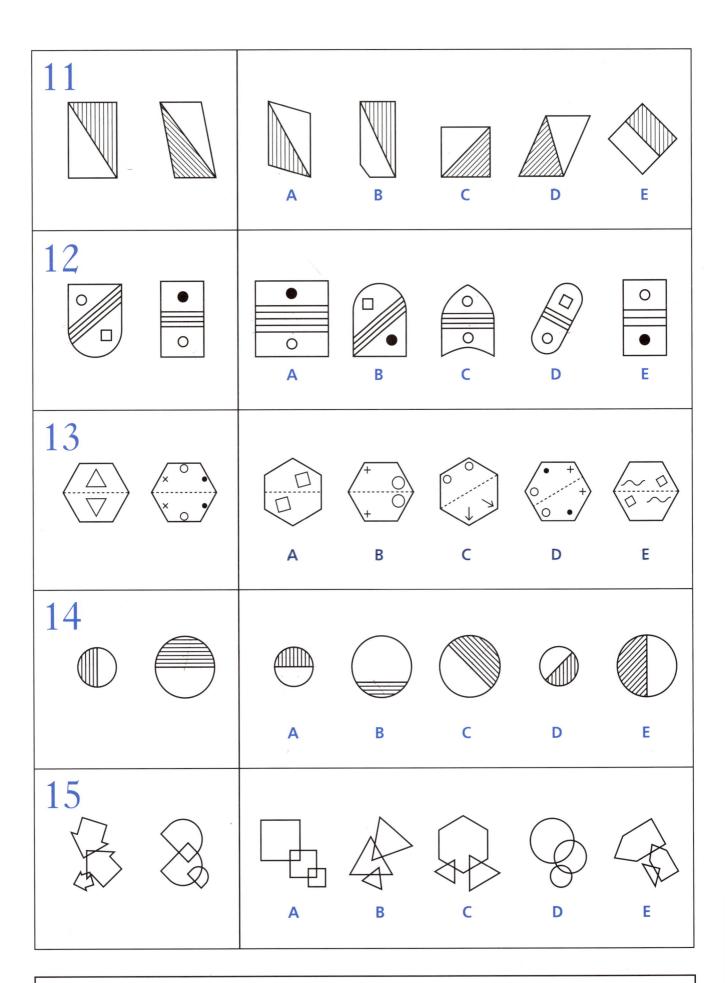

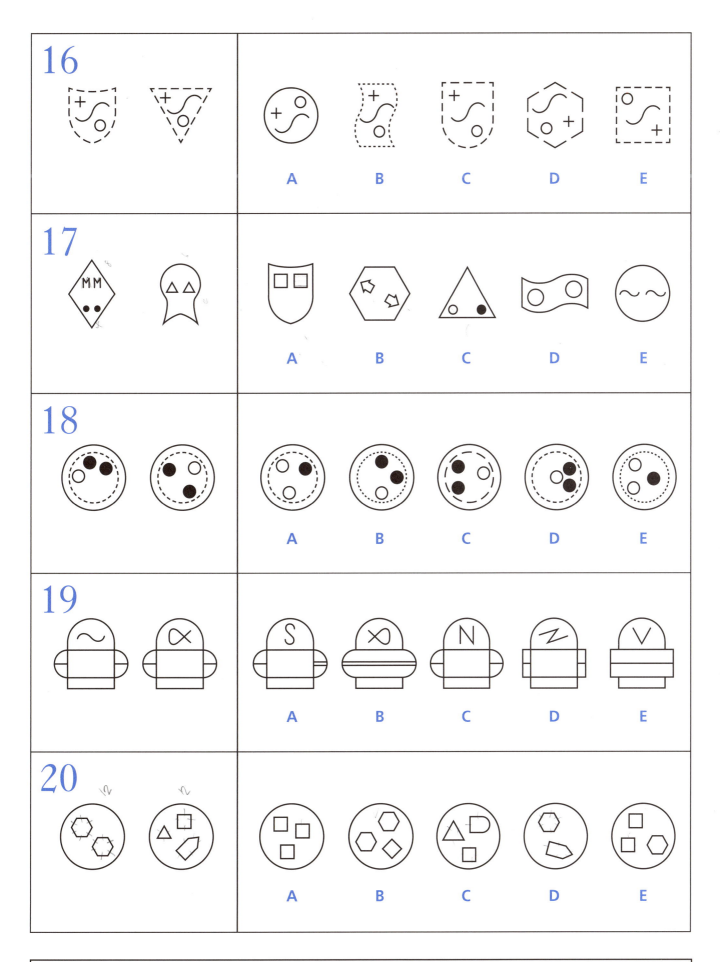

Do not turn over until you are told to do so

Please go on to the next page >>>

The big square on the left in the example below contains four small squares. One of the small squares has been left empty. One of the five figures on the right should fill the empty square. Its letter has been marked on your answer sheet.

**Example**

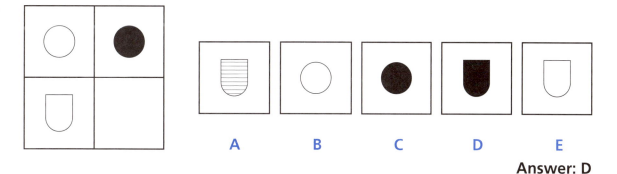

**Answer: D**

Now do the two practice questions below.
**Mark the correct answers on your answer sheet.**

## P1

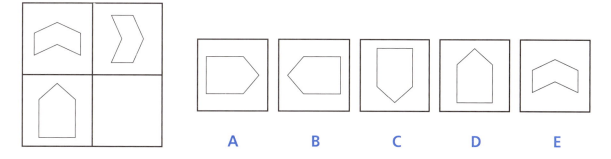

## P2

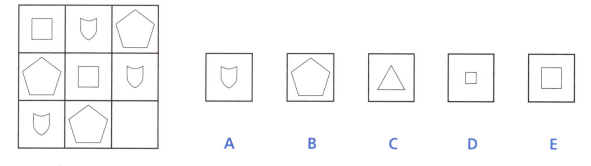

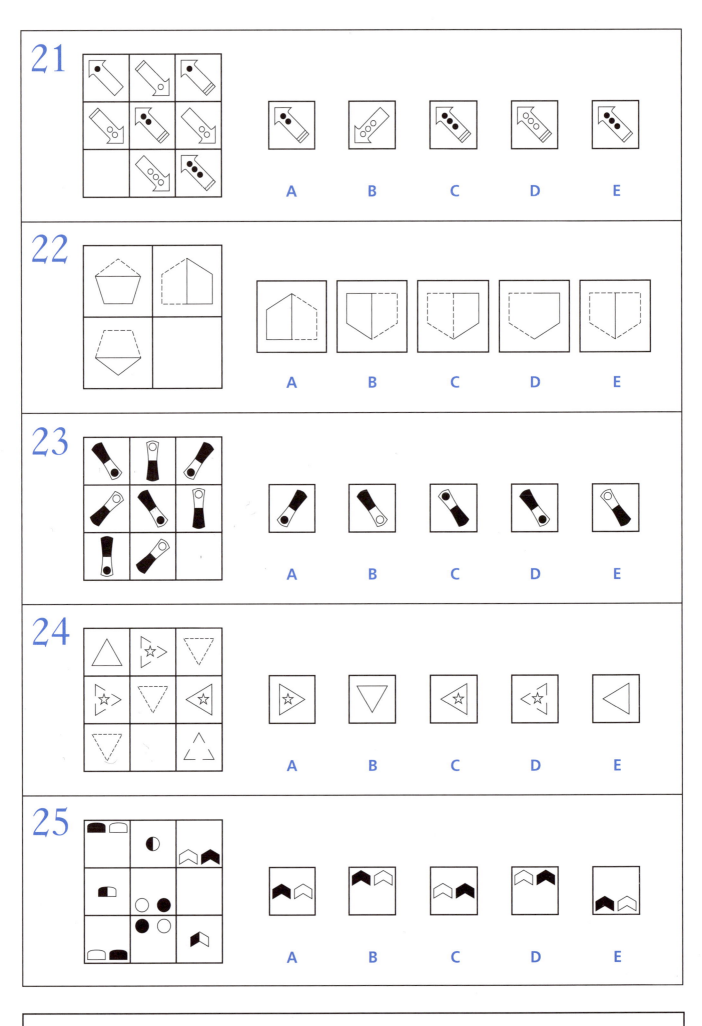

21

A  B  C  D  E

22

A  B  C  D  E

23

A  B  C  D  E

24

A  B  C  D  E

25

A  B  C  D  E

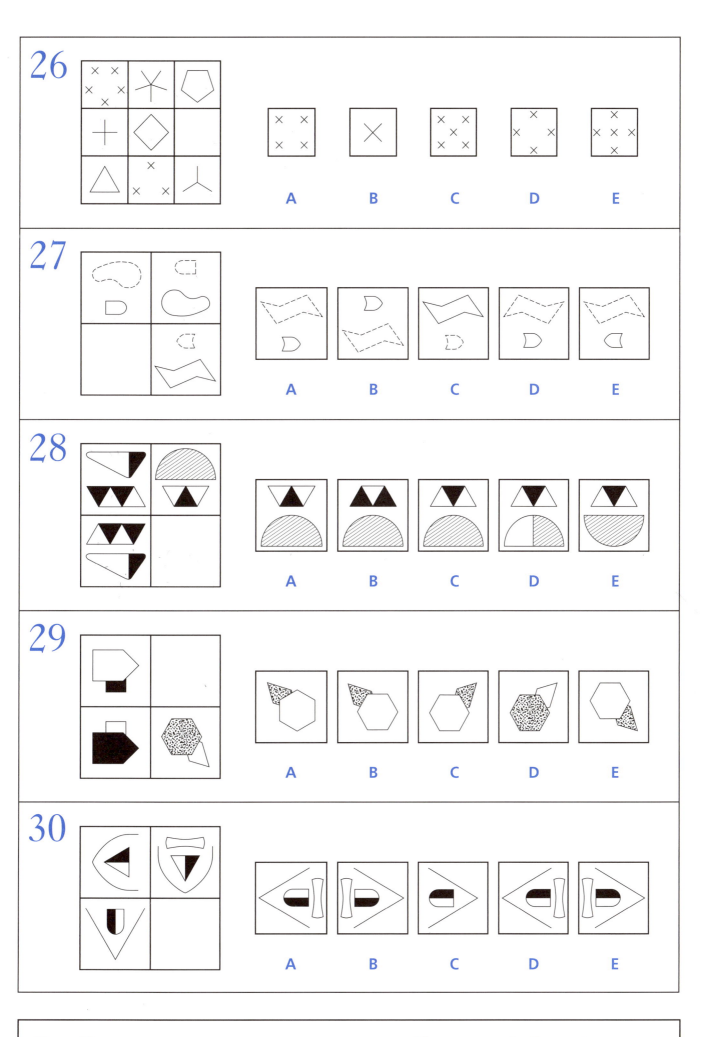

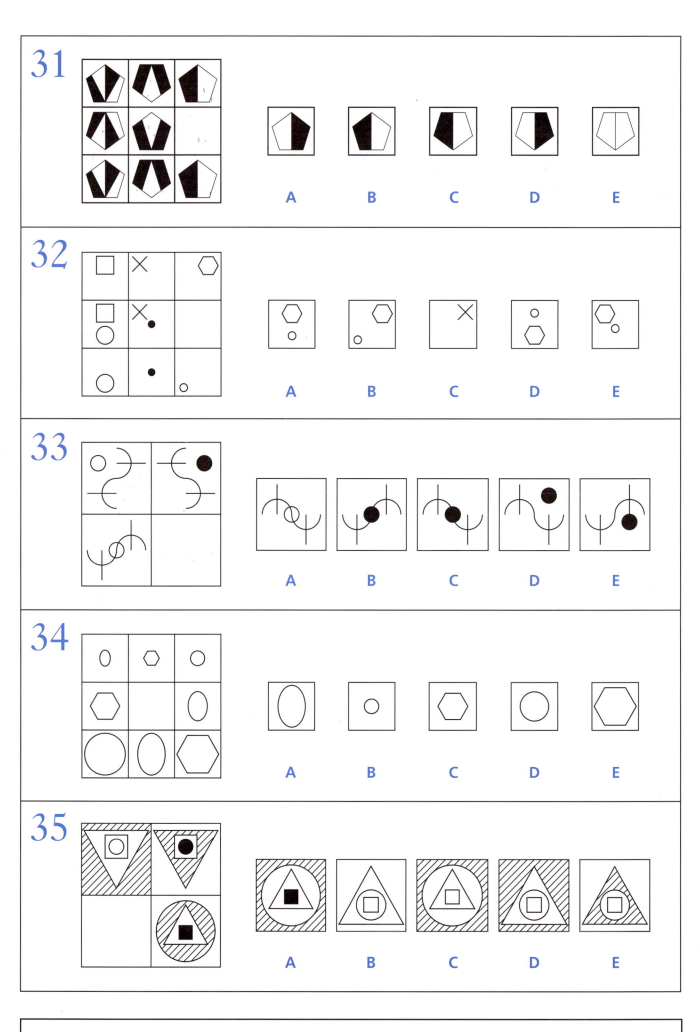

31

A   B   C   D   E

32

A   B   C   D   E

33

A   B   C   D   E

34

A   B   C   D   E

35

A   B   C   D   E

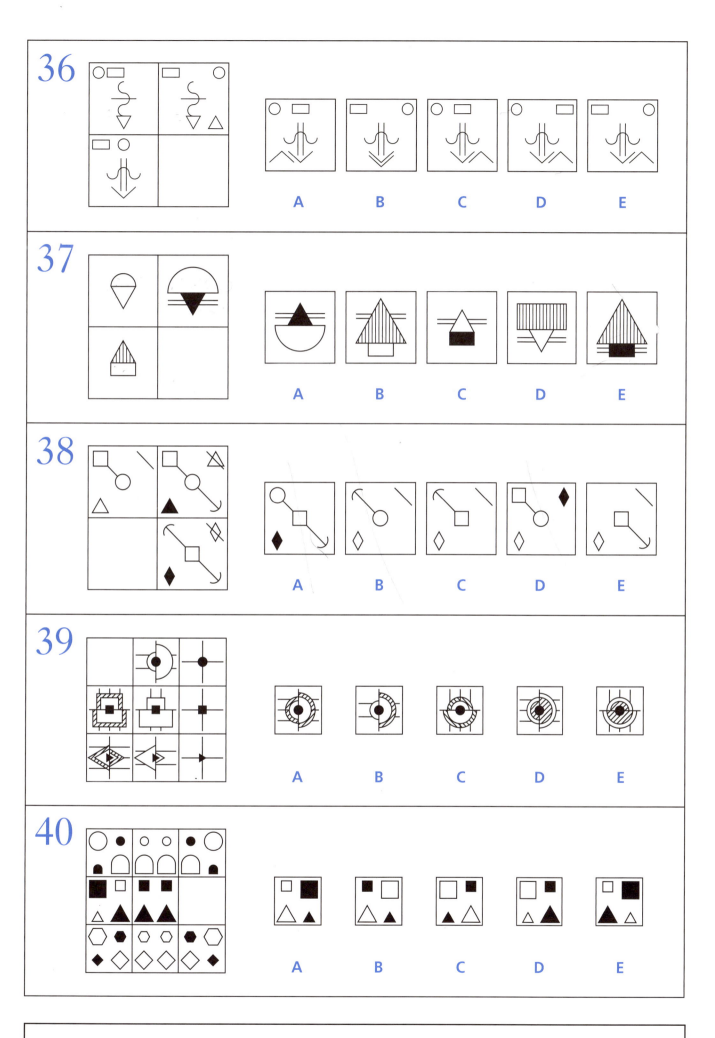

36

37

38

39

40

A      B      C      D      E

# Practice Paper 2

# Non-Verbal Reasoning

## Read the following carefully:

1. **Do not open or turn over the page in this booklet until you are told to do so.**

2. This is a multiple-choice test in which you have to mark your answer to each question on the answer sheet. You should mark only one answer for each question.

3. Draw a firm line clearly through the rectangle next to your answer like this ▭. If you make a mistake, rub it out as completely as you can and put in your new answer.

4. There are two sections in this test. Each section starts with an explanation of what to do, followed by a worked example with the answer marked on the answer sheet. Each section also contains some practice questions.

5. Be sure to keep your place in the correct section on the answer sheet. Mark your answer in the box that has the same number as the test question.

6. You may not be able to finish all the questions, but try to do as many as you can. If you cannot do a question, do not waste time on it but go on to the next. If you are not sure of an answer, choose the one you think is best.

7. You may do any rough working on a separate sheet of paper.

8. **Work as quickly and as carefully as you can.**

Please go on to the next page >>>

In the example below, there are five figures. One of these figures is **most unlike** the other four and its letter has been marked on your answer sheet.

**Example**

A B C D E

**Answer: B**

Now do the two practice questions below.
**Mark the correct answers on your answer sheet.**

## P1

A B C D E

## P2

A B C D E

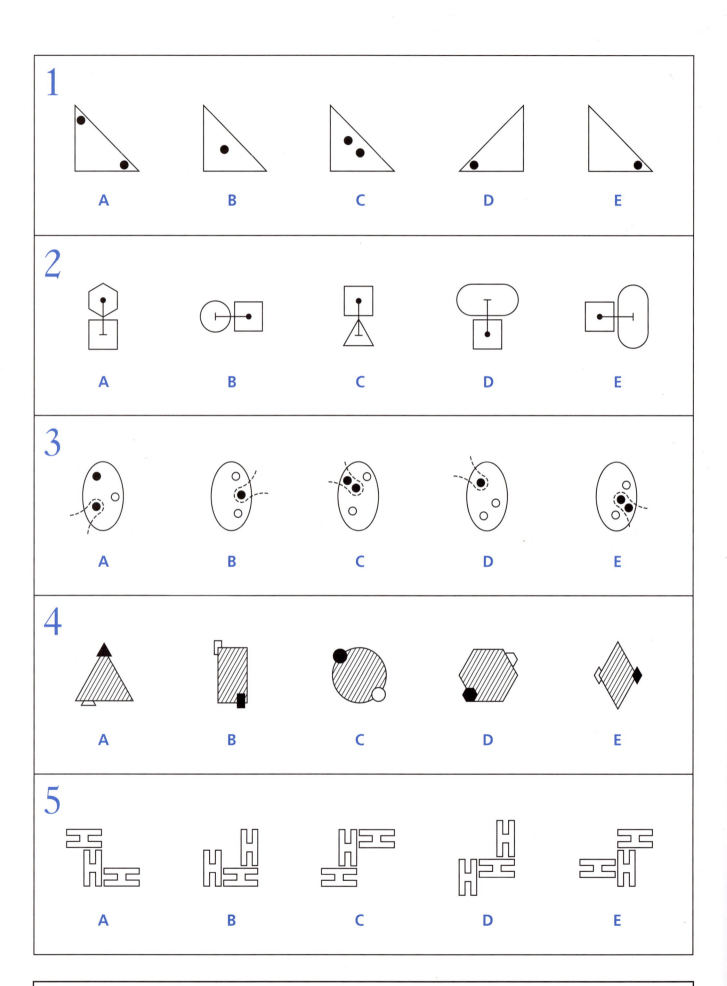

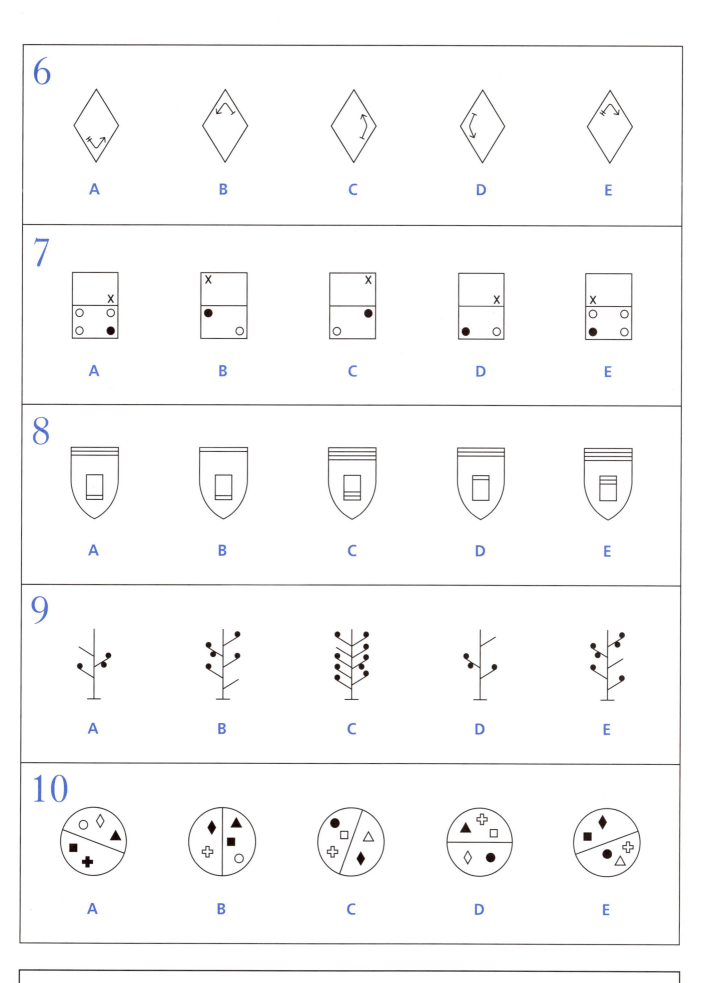

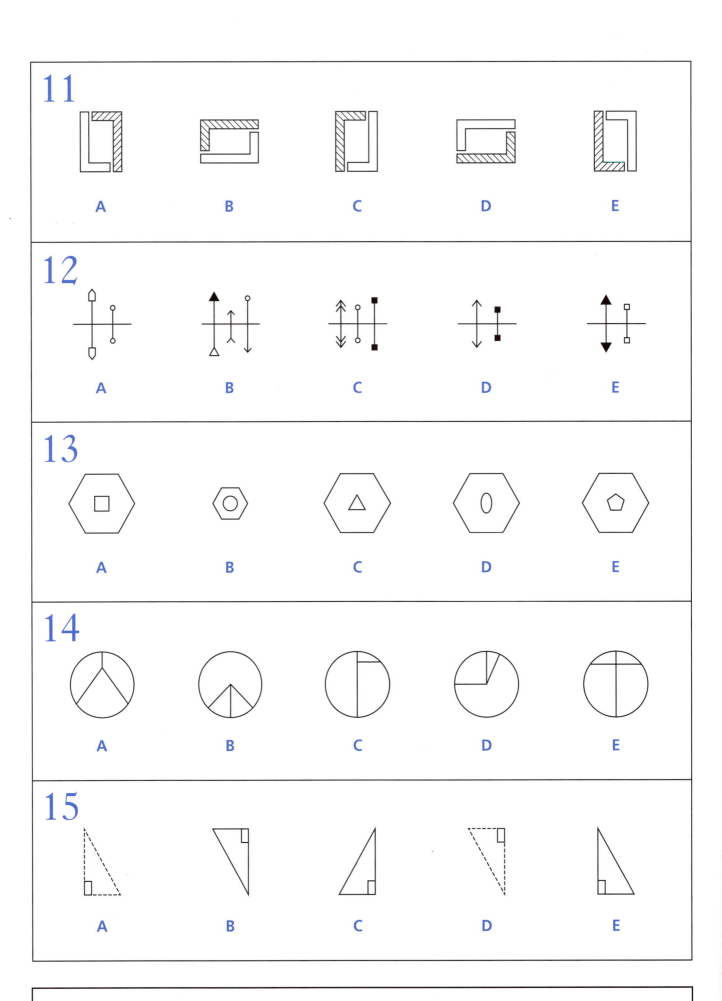

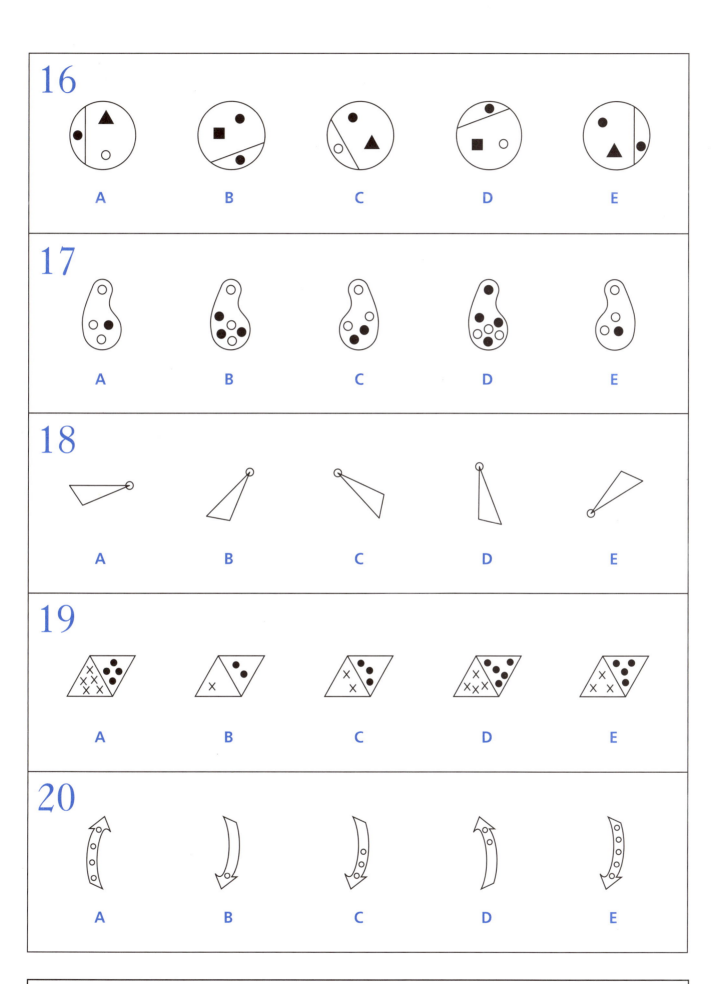

Please go on to the next page >>>

On the left in the example below, there are two shapes with an arrow between them. Decide how the second shape is related to the first. After these there is a third shape, then an arrow and then five more shapes. Decide which of the five shapes goes with the **third** one to **make a pair** like the two on the left. Its letter has been marked on your answer sheet.

**Example**

A    B    C    D    E

**Answer: B**

Now do the two practice questions below.
**Mark the correct answers on your answer sheet.**

## P1

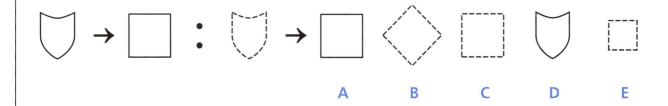

A    B    C    D    E

## P2

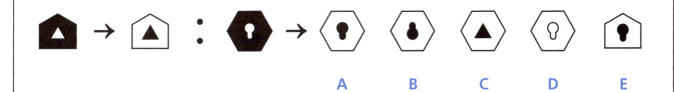

A    B    C    D    E

## 21

A     B     C     D     E

## 22

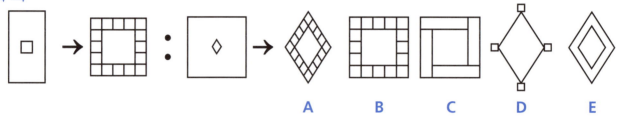

A     B     C     D     E

## 23

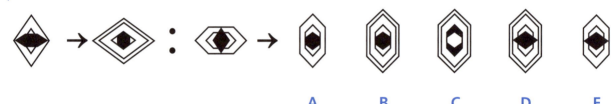

A     B     C     D     E

## 24

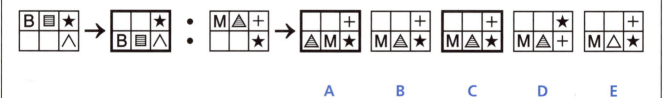

A     B     C     D     E

## 25

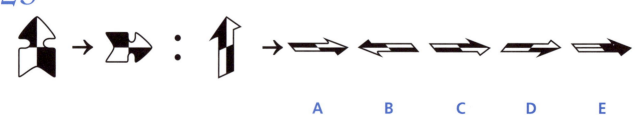

A     B     C     D     E

**26**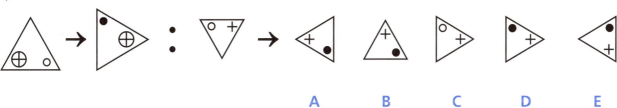

                                        A         B         C         D         E

**27**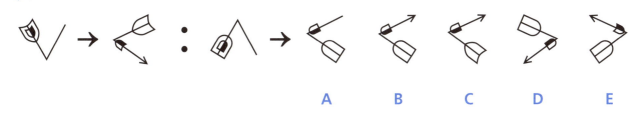

                                        A         B         C         D         E

**28**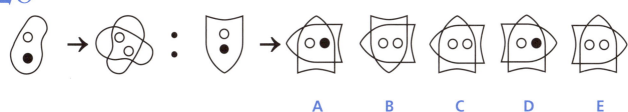

                                        A         B         C         D         E

**29**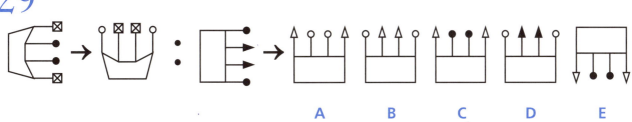

                                        A         B         C         D         E

**30**

                                        A         B         C         D         E

## 31

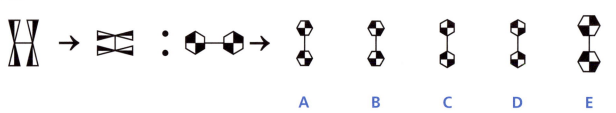

A     B     C     D     E

## 32

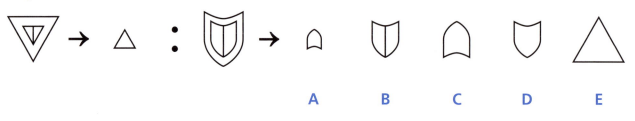

A     B     C     D     E

## 33

A     B     C     D     E

## 34

A     B     C     D     E

## 35

A     B     C     D     E

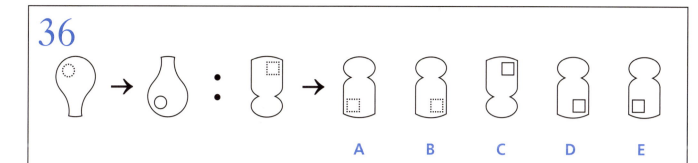

## 36

A     B     C     D     E

## 37

A     B     C     D     E

## 38

A     B     C     D     E

## 39

A     B     C     D     E

## 40

A     B     C     D     E

Published by GL Assessment, 1st Floor, Vantage London, Great West Road, Brentford TW8 9AG.

Printed in China.

Code 6802 017
1(11.18) PF

# Practice Paper 3

## Non-Verbal Reasoning

**Read the following carefully:**

1. **Do not open or turn over the page in this booklet until you are told to do so.**

2. This is a multiple-choice test in which you have to mark your answer to each question on the answer sheet. You should mark only one answer for each question.

3. Draw a firm line clearly through the rectangle next to your answer like this ▭. If you make a mistake, rub it out as completely as you can and put in your new answer.

4. There are two sections in this test. Each section starts with an explanation of what to do, followed by a worked example with the answer marked on the answer sheet. Each section also contains some practice questions.

5. Be sure to keep your place in the correct section on the answer sheet. Mark your answer in the box that has the same number as the test question.

6. You may not be able to finish all the questions, but try to do as many as you can. If you cannot do a question, do not waste time on it but go on to the next. If you are not sure of an answer, choose the one you think is best.

7. You may do any rough working on a separate sheet of paper.

8. **Work as quickly and as carefully as you can.**

Please go on to the next page >>>

To answer these questions, you have to work out a code. In the boxes on the left, there are shapes and the code letters that go with them. The top letters mean something different from the bottom ones. You must decide how the letters go with the shapes. Then find the correct code for the **test shape** from the set of five codes on the right and **mark its letter on your answer sheet**. The examples below have been done for you and the answers marked on the answer sheet.

**Example 1**

TEST SHAPE

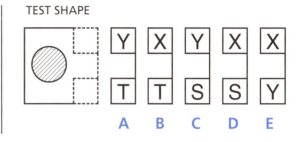

A   B   C   D   E

**Answer: B**

In the example above, both squares have a Y at the top but the circle has an X, so the top code must be for shape. Both white shapes have an S at the bottom, but the shaded shape has a T, so the bottom code must be for shading. The test shape is a shaded circle so its code letters must be X for circle and T for shading, and **B** has been marked on the answer sheet. Now look at the second example:

**Example 2**

TEST SHAPE

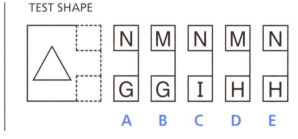

A   B   C   D   E

**Answer: A**

Both circles have an M at the top but the triangle has an N, so the top code must be for shape. The bottom code letter is different for each shape so G, H and I must be the codes for no dot, one dot and two dots. The test shape is a triangle with no dots so its code letters must be N for triangle and G for no dots, and **A** has been marked on the answer sheet.

Now do the practice question below and **mark the correct answer on your answer sheet**. **Remember there is a new code for each question.**

## P1

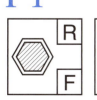     

A   B   C   D   E

## 1

| | A | B | C | D | E |
|---|---|---|---|---|---|
| | G | F | H | G | F |
| | Q | Q | Q | P | P |

## 2

| | A | B | C | D | E |
|---|---|---|---|---|---|
| | W | V | W | V | W |
| | F | F | H | H | G |

## 3

| | A | B | C | D | E |
|---|---|---|---|---|---|
| | M | L | K | L | M |
| | H | H | G | G | G |

## 4

| | A | B | C | D | E |
|---|---|---|---|---|---|
| | F | G | H | G | H |
| | T | S | U | U | S |

## 5

| | A | B | C | D | E |
|---|---|---|---|---|---|
| | W | W | X | X | Y |
| | L | K | K | L | J |

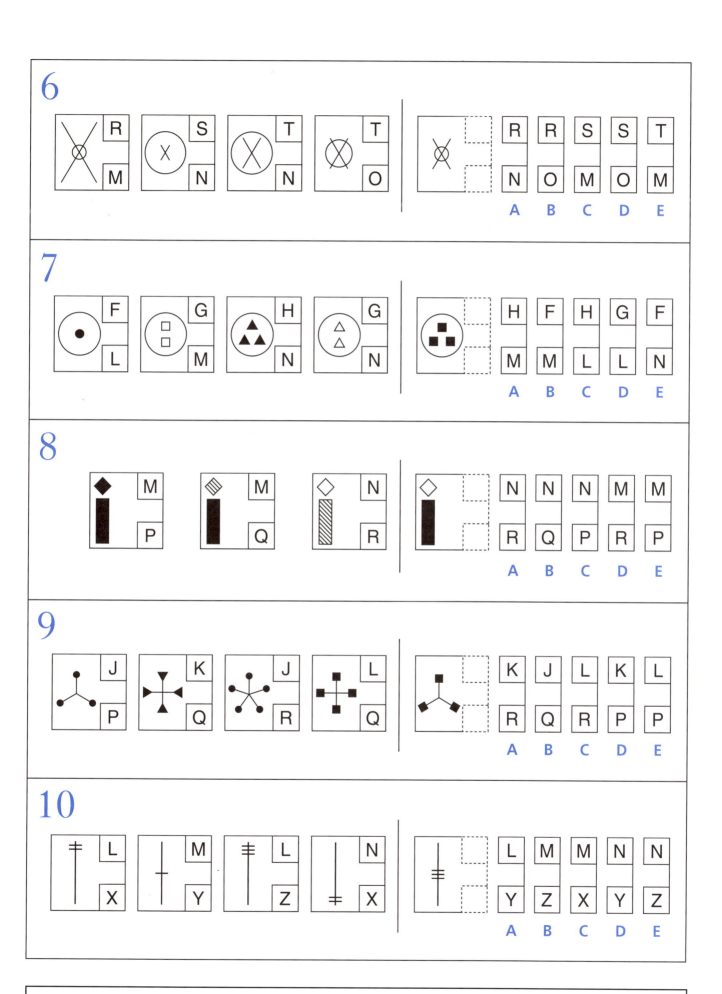

**6**

|  | A | B | C | D | E |
|---|---|---|---|---|---|
| | R | R | S | S | T |
| | N | O | M | O | M |

**7**

|  | A | B | C | D | E |
|---|---|---|---|---|---|
| | H | F | H | G | F |
| | M | M | L | L | N |

**8**

|  | A | B | C | D | E |
|---|---|---|---|---|---|
| | N | N | N | M | M |
| | R | Q | P | R | P |

**9**

|  | A | B | C | D | E |
|---|---|---|---|---|---|
| | K | J | L | K | L |
| | R | Q | R | P | P |

**10**

|  | A | B | C | D | E |
|---|---|---|---|---|---|
| | L | M | M | N | N |
| | Y | Z | X | Y | Z |

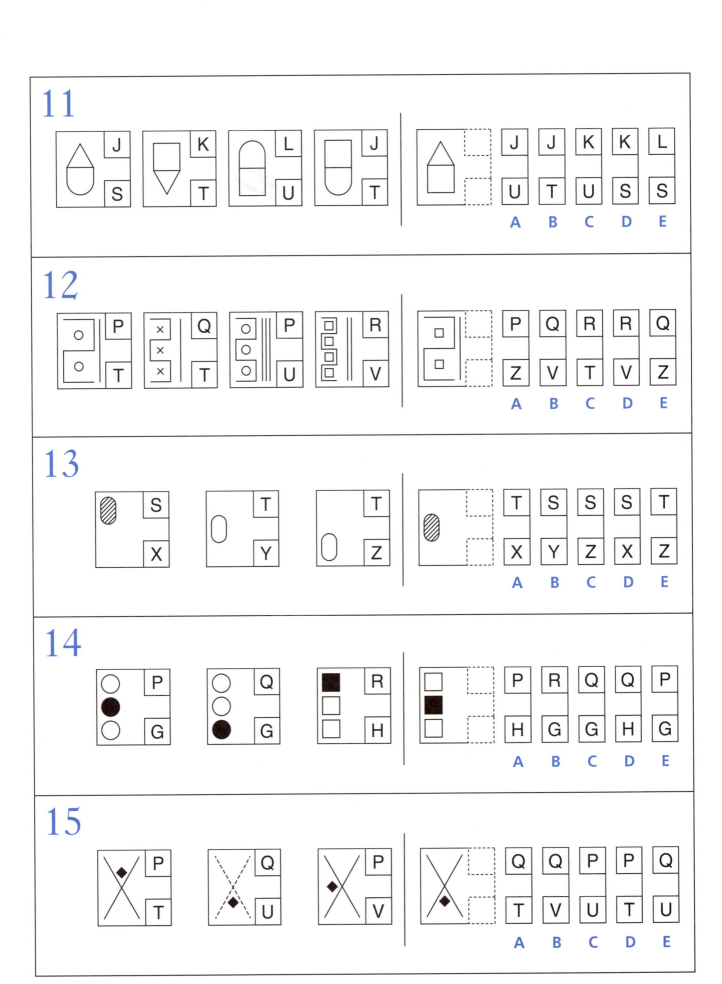

Please go on to the next page >>>

**16**

| U | S | T | T | U |
|---|---|---|---|---|
| J | L | L | J | K |
| A | B | C | D | E |

**17**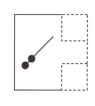

| M | K | K | L | M |
|---|---|---|---|---|
| W | X | Y | Y | X |
| A | B | C | D | E |

**18**

| X | W | Y | X | Y |
|---|---|---|---|---|
| R | Q | R | P | P |
| A | B | C | D | E |

**19**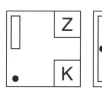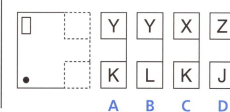

| Y | Y | X | Z | Z |
|---|---|---|---|---|
| K | L | K | J | L |
| A | B | C | D | E |

**20**

| M | O | N | M | O |
|---|---|---|---|---|
| Y | X | W | X | Y |
| A | B | C | D | E |

Please go on to the next page >>>

# Section 2

On the left in the example below, there are five squares arranged in order. One of these squares has been left empty. One of the five squares on the right should **take the place** of the empty square and its letter has been marked on your answer sheet.

**Example**

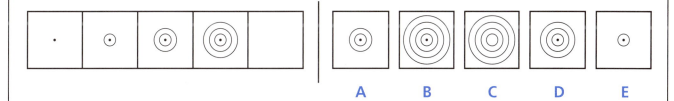

A    B    C    D    E

**Answer: B**

Now do the two practice questions below.
**Mark the correct answers on your answer sheet.**

## P1

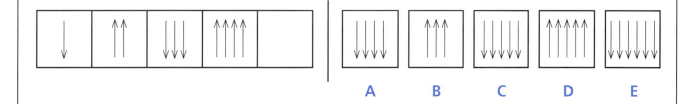

A    B    C    D    E

## P2

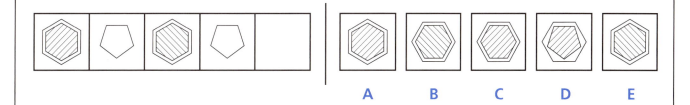

A    B    C    D    E

## 21

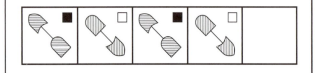     

A    B    C    D    E

## 22

A    B    C    D    E

## 23

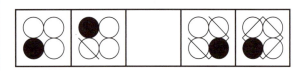     

A    B    C    D    E

## 24

A    B    C    D    E

## 25

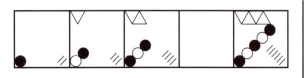     

A    B    C    D    E

**26**

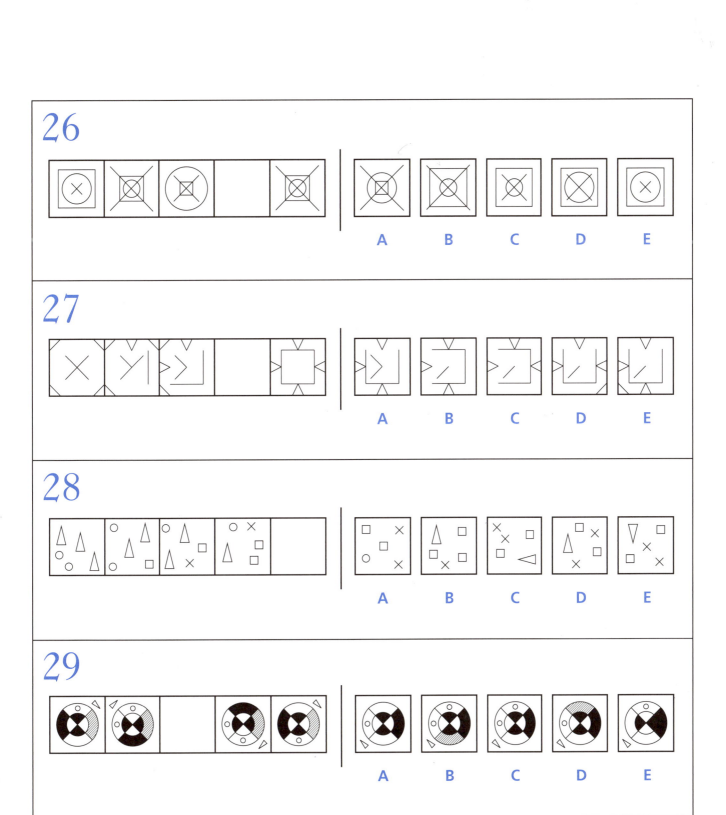

**27**

**28**

**29**

**30**

**31**

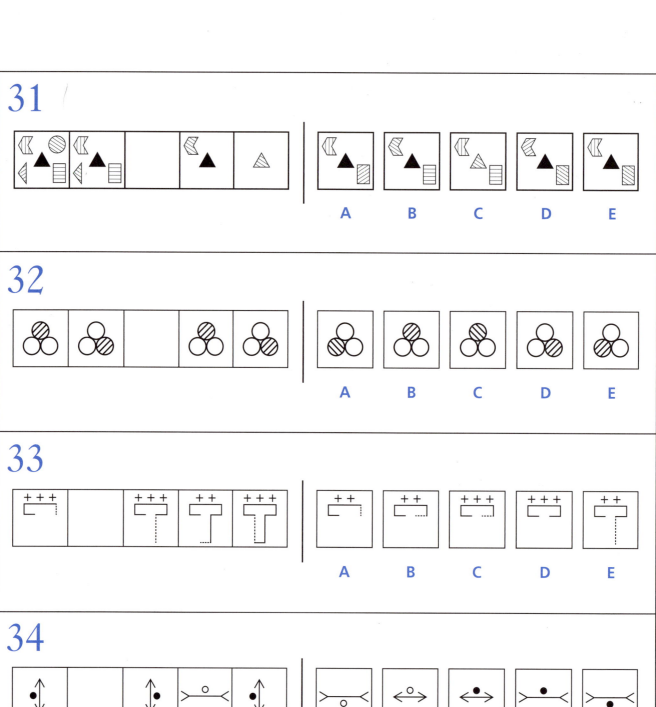

A    B    C    D    E

**32**

A    B    C    D    E

**33**

A    B    C    D    E

**34**

A    B    C    D    E

**35**

A    B    C    D    E

**36**

A　B　C　D　E

**37**

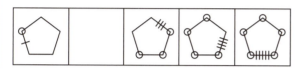　

A　B　C　D　E

**38**

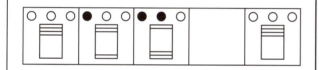　

A　B　C　D　E

**39**

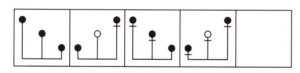　

A　B　C　D　E

**40**

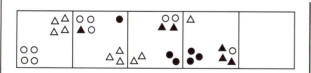　

A　B　C　D　E

Published by GL Assessment, 1st Floor, Vantage London, Great West Road, Brentford TW8 9AG.

Printed in China.

Code 6802 018
1(11.18) PF

# Notes and Answers for Parents

# Non-Verbal Reasoning Pack 1

11+ Practice Papers

GL Assessment®

# Introduction

## About the Tests

These tests are designed to give your child practice in sitting a formal type of examination before they take the actual 11+ test.

The papers are presented in a very similar way to many of the test papers used for selection at 11+, and the questions represent the type of questions used, although they may not be exactly the same level of difficulty. Therefore, your child's scores on these tests will not necessarily be a direct indication of their likely score on an actual 11+ test. Furthermore, the pass marks for the actual test will depend, to some extent, on the overall standard of the candidates.

## Preparation for Testing

Give your child the test at an appropriate time, when they are both physically and mentally alert. Choose a suitable area for them to work in – make sure they can work comfortably and are free from any distractions.

Before your child takes a practice test, discuss with them the reasons why they are doing the test. Also, explain that they might find some of the questions difficult, but that they should work as quickly and as carefully as they can. If they get stuck on a question, they should not waste too much time on it but move on to the next one. If they have time left at the end, they can go back to it then.

# Taking the Tests

Your child should record their answers in the Answer Sheets booklet provided – not in the test booklet. Answer Sheets are provided for all three tests in this pack.

The actual 11+ test will be marked by a computer, but you will need to score the practice tests yourself using the Answer Key in this booklet. It is important for your child to learn how to use the Answer Sheets properly, in preparation for the real test: they should record an answer in the appropriate box by drawing a clear line through it with a pencil. Mistakes should be rubbed out carefully and **not** crossed out, since in the actual test this would not be recorded correctly by the computer. You can ignore the boxes at the top marked 'Pupil Number', 'School Number' and 'Date of Birth'. These need to be filled in only for the actual test. By encountering these features now, your child will be more familiar with the style of the actual 11+ paper when they take the test.

**Ways to Do the Test Session**

The tests have two separate sections. Each section is preceded by instructions on how to answer the questions, one or two examples and some practice questions. This is then followed by 20 test questions.

In the actual exam, the invigilator will read these instructions aloud to candidates.

There are three main ways you can do the Non-Verbal Reasoning tests at home:

1. **a.** Turn to Section 1 of the test booklet with your child. Read through the example at the top together. Then ask your child to do the practice questions, giving them the answers to these when they have finished (see Answer Key). Finally, time them for 10 minutes on the following 20 questions.

   **b.** If your child has not finished the 20 questions after 10 minutes, draw a line underneath the question they are on, or draw a ring around its number, and then let them carry on until they have completed the section. When you mark the test, you will be able to see how many questions your child got right in the allocated time and how many questions overall. This will give you a good indication of whether they need to develop their speed and/or work more accurately.

   **c.** Repeat this procedure for the second section.

OR

2. **a.** Ask your child to read through the example in Section 1 by themselves and do the practice questions, then give them the answers (see Answer Key). They should tell you when they are ready to begin the timed section. You should then time them for 10 minutes on the following 20 questions.

   **b.** As above for option 1.

   **c.** As above for option 1.

OR

3. **a.** You can simply give the test to your child and ask them to read through and complete it on their own, with no help, involvement or timing on your part. In this case you will not be able to give them the answers to the practice questions until they have finished the whole test. You should tell them to ignore the instructions stating 'Do not turn over until you are told to do so'.

Please note, if you want your child to experience the test as closely as possible to the real test, you should choose option 1. The test should take around 30 minutes in total, including practice questions.

# Marking and Feedback

The answers are provided on pages 5–7. Only these answers are allowed. One mark should be given for each correct answer – do not allow half marks or 'the benefit of the doubt'. Do not deduct marks for wrong answers.

The results may suggest that more practice is needed. Always try to be positive and encouraging. Talk through the mistakes your child has made in a constructive way. Work out together how to get the right answer.

# Answer Key

**Practice Paper 1**

Section 1

| Question | Answer |
|----------|--------|
| **P1** | B |
| **P2** | C |
| **1** | B |
| **2** | D |
| **3** | C |
| **4** | C |
| **5** | D |
| **6** | B |
| **7** | A |
| **8** | A |
| **9** | A |
| **10** | C |
| **11** | D |
| **12** | C |
| **13** | B |
| **14** | C |
| **15** | B |
| **16** | C |
| **17** | A |
| **18** | D |
| **19** | C |
| **20** | A |

Section 2

| Question | Answer |
|----------|--------|
| **P1** | A |
| **P2** | E |
| **21** | C |
| **22** | B |
| **23** | D |
| **24** | C |
| **25** | B |
| **26** | D |
| **27** | A |
| **28** | B |
| **29** | C |
| **30** | E |
| **31** | C |
| **32** | B |
| **33** | C |
| **34** | D |
| **35** | C |
| **36** | D |
| **37** | E |
| **38** | C |
| **39** | A |
| **40** | E |

# Answer Key

**Practice Paper 2**

Section 1

| Question | Answer |
| --- | --- |
| **P1** | C |
| **P2** | D |
| **1** | D |
| **2** | A |
| **3** | A |
| **4** | C |
| **5** | E |
| **6** | E |
| **7** | D |
| **8** | B |
| **9** | E |
| **10** | A |
| **11** | C |
| **12** | B |
| **13** | B |
| **14** | E |
| **15** | C |
| **16** | C |
| **17** | D |
| **18** | D |
| **19** | A |
| **20** | D |

Section 2

| Question | Answer |
| --- | --- |
| **P1** | C |
| **P2** | A |
| **21** | A |
| **22** | A |
| **23** | B |
| **24** | C |
| **25** | A |
| **26** | A |
| **27** | D |
| **28** | C |
| **29** | C |
| **30** | A |
| **31** | A |
| **32** | C |
| **33** | A |
| **34** | D |
| **35** | C |
| **36** | D |
| **37** | B |
| **38** | D |
| **39** | C |
| **40** | E |

# Answer Key

**Practice Paper 3**

## Section 1

| Question | Answer |
|---|---|
| **P1** | E |
| **1** | B |
| **2** | A |
| **3** | D |
| **4** | C |
| **5** | B |
| **6** | E |
| **7** | A |
| **8** | D |
| **9** | E |
| **10** | B |
| **11** | E |
| **12** | C |
| **13** | B |
| **14** | A |
| **15** | C |
| **16** | D |
| **17** | A |
| **18** | C |
| **19** | A |
| **20** | D |

## Section 2

| Question | Answer |
|---|---|
| **P1** | C |
| **P2** | A |
| **21** | C |
| **22** | B |
| **23** | B |
| **24** | C |
| **25** | C |
| **26** | E |
| **27** | E |
| **28** | D |
| **29** | A |
| **30** | C |
| **31** | E |
| **32** | E |
| **33** | B |
| **34** | A |
| **35** | C |
| **36** | D |
| **37** | B |
| **38** | D |
| **39** | E |
| **40** | D |

# Answer Sheets

# Non-Verbal Reasoning
## Practice Papers 1–3

This booklet contains the answer sheets needed for Non-Verbal Reasoning Practice Papers 1–3.

Please make sure you use the correct answer sheet for the test being taken, following the title at the top of each page.

The following answer sheets are included:

Non-Verbal Reasoning Practice Paper 1
Non-Verbal Reasoning Practice Paper 2
Non-Verbal Reasoning Practice Paper 3

11+ Practice Papers

GL Assessment®

Published by GL Assessment, 1st Floor, Vantage London, Great West Road,
Brentford TW8 9AG.

Printed in China.

Code 6802 020
1(11.18) PF

# NON-VERBAL REASONING PRACTICE PAPER 1

GL Assessment®

| Pupil's Name |
|---|
| School Name |

| DATE OF TEST | | |
|---|---|---|
| Day | Month | Year |
| | | |

| UNIQUE PUPIL NUMBER |
|---|
| |

| SCHOOL NUMBER |
|---|
| |

| DATE OF BIRTH | | |
|---|---|---|
| Day | Month | Year |
| | | |

Please mark boxes with a thin horizontal line like this ▬.

## SECTION 1

EXAMPLE
A
B
C ▬
D
E

P1: A B C D E

P2: A B C D E

1: A B C D E
2: A B C D E
3: A B C D E
4: A B C D E
5: A B C D E
6: A B C D E
7: A B C D E
8: A B C D E
9: A B C D E
10: A B C D E
11: A B C D E
12: A B C D E
13: A B C D E
14: A B C D E
15: A B C D E
16: A B C D E
17: A B C D E
18: A B C D E
19: A B C D E
20: A B C D E

## SECTION 2

EXAMPLE
A
B
C
D ▬
E

P1: A B C D E

P2: A B C D E

21: A B C D E
22: A B C D E
23: A B C D E
24: A B C D E
25: A B C D E
26: A B C D E
27: A B C D E
28: A B C D E
29: A B C D E
30: A B C D E
31: A B C D E
32: A B C D E
33: A B C D E
34: A B C D E
35: A B C D E
36: A B C D E
37: A B C D E
38: A B C D E
39: A B C D E
40: A B C D E

11+NVR-1

END OF TEST

# NON-VERBAL REASONING PRACTICE PAPER 2

| Pupil's Name | DATE OF TEST |
| --- | --- |
| School Name | Day / Month / Year |

| UNIQUE PUPIL NUMBER | SCHOOL NUMBER | DATE OF BIRTH |
| --- | --- | --- |
| | | Day / Month / Year |

Please mark boxes with a thin horizontal line like this ▬.

## SECTION 1

EXAMPLE
A ☐
B ▬
C ☐
D ☐
E ☐

P1
A ☐
B ☐
C ☐
D ☐
E ☐

P2
A ☐
B ☐
C ☐
D ☐
E ☐

Questions 1–20 (A, B, C, D, E answer boxes)

## SECTION 2

EXAMPLE
A ☐
B ▬
C ☐
D ☐
E ☐

P1
A ☐
B ☐
C ☐
D ☐
E ☐

P2
A ☐
B ☐
C ☐
D ☐
E ☐

Questions 21–40 (A, B, C, D, E answer boxes)

**END OF TEST**

# NON-VERBAL REASONING PRACTICE PAPER 3

**Pupil's Name**

**School Name**

**DATE OF TEST**
| Day | Month | Year |
|---|---|---|

**UNIQUE PUPIL NUMBER**

**SCHOOL NUMBER**

**DATE OF BIRTH**
| Day | Month | Year |
|---|---|---|

Please mark boxes with a thin horizontal line like this ▬.

## SECTION 1

EXAMPLE 1
A
B ▬
C
D
E

EXAMPLE 2
A ▬
B
C
D
E

P1
A
B
C
D
E

1  A B C D E
2  A B C D E
3  A B C D E
4  A B C D E
5  A B C D E
6  A B C D E
7  A B C D E

8  A B C D E
9  A B C D E
10 A B C D E
11 A B C D E
12 A B C D E
13 A B C D E
14 A B C D E

15 A B C D E
16 A B C D E
17 A B C D E
18 A B C D E
19 A B C D E
20 A B C D E

## SECTION 2

EXAMPLE
A
B ▬
C
D
E

P1
A
B
C
D
E

P2
A
B
C
D
E

21 A B C D E
22 A B C D E
23 A B C D E
24 A B C D E
25 A B C D E
26 A B C D E
27 A B C D E

28 A B C D E
29 A B C D E
30 A B C D E
31 A B C D E
32 A B C D E
33 A B C D E
34 A B C D E

35 A B C D E
36 A B C D E
37 A B C D E
38 A B C D E
39 A B C D E
40 A B C D E

11+NVR-3

# END OF TEST